# Wit and Humour in Modern China
## —100 Cartoons by Ding Cong

Bilingual Edition

NEW WORLD PRESS
Beijing, China

## CONTENTS

Ding Cong and His Cartoons
 *by Gladys Yang and Yang Xianyi*     5

Cartoons and Modern Tales     12

List of Titles     212

## Ding Cong and His Cartoons

In 1985 Ding Cong published a collection of his cartoons entitled *Wit and Humour from Ancient China*. It ridicules stupid officials, pokes fun at pretensions or follies and records smart repartee, displaying much the same style of humour throughout two millennia. The book was very well received. Readers have been suggesting that the artist should produce another collection of cartoons reflecting the ignorance, stupidity and other irrational phenomena that still exist in present-day Chinese society; so this present collection *Wit and Humour in Modern China* is a sister volume to the former book.

Seven years have passed since the publication of the former volume, and Ding Cong is now seventy-six. He still enjoys good health and works hard, still signs his work Little Ding. He first did so in his teens to distinguish himself from his father Ding Song, a veteran cartoonist in Shanghai. Ding Song's home was frequented by actors, writers and painters, and from his boyhood Little Ding loved art. But an artist's life was so hard in those days that his father did not want him to follow his steps; he refused to teach him. Art was the youngster's hobby and he learned from life, taking a sketch-book with him wherever he went. His only formal training was a term of drawing classes at the Shanghai Fine Arts Institute.

Like virtually all Chinese artists of his generation Ding Cong has had a very chequered career. The Anti-Japanese War forced him to move from Shanghai to the interior. Later, Kuomintang censorship and persecution of radicals drove him from Shanghai to Hong Kong. After Liberation the Anti-Rightist Movement and the "cultural revolution" robbed him for twenty years of the freedom to publish under his own name. Under these circumstances it is amazing that he has achieved so much. On the other hand, the ups and downs of his life have toughened him, enriched his experience and deepened his sympathy for all underdogs.

Ding Cong started his career by drawing cartoons and helping to edit film magazines and pictorials. In the interior and Hong Kong he also designed stage sets and costumes experience which stands him in good stead when illustrating stories from the past. After the outbreak of the Pacific War in 1942, he went back to the interior and contributed to the exhibition "Hong Kong in Torment." His travels with a repertory company brought him in touch with social outcasts, whose sufferings he often took as his theme. Thus his *The Red Light District* and other drawings of social phenomena portray the hard life of prostitutes in Chengdu as well as the rampant corruption in wartime China. In recognition of his outstanding work he was made a member of the Modern Art Association.

In 1944 he drew brilliant illustrations for Lu Xun's masterpiece *The True Story of Ah Q*, satirizing the landlord and Imitation Foreign Devil but showing sympathy for feckless Ah Q, considering him as a victim of his times. This sympathy for the poor and ignorant pervades all his illustrations.

Returning to Shanghai in 1945, and later when he returned to Hong Kong, Ding Cong drew cartoons attacking the Kuomintang's reactionary regime. "Cartoons can be compared to daggers," he said. "Armed with them I have pierced through dark and gloomy times."

After Liberation Ding Cong came to Beijing, became an editor of the *China Pictorial*, drew cartoons, illustrated stories and helped to design exhibitions. One of our earliest recollections of him is when, like a smiling Buddha, he showed us round the fascinating exhibition of the classical novel *A Dream of Red Mansions* which he had been instrumental in arranging. The wealth of material assembled shed light on the novel and its historical background, the costumes and furnishings of that time, even the tricks resorted to by desperate candidates to cheat in the imperial examinations.... That was one of the best exhibitions we have seen.

In 1957, wrongly labelled as a Rightist, Ding Cong was sent to the Great Northern Waste to work on the land. Though the temperature sometimes dropped to 30 degrees below zero, he never complained but retained his sense of humour. In 1960 he was cleared and given a job in the National Art Gallery. But in 1966 came the "cultural revolution," he was sent to a cadre school and then to the countryside to work as a swineherd.

When rehabilitated in 1979, Ding Cong determined to make up for lost time. His work is in great demand. His cartoons keep appearing in papers and magazines. He has illustrated many books by such famous writers as Lu Xun, Lao She and Mao Dun, as well as many others. After making a careful study of these works he faithfully reflects and illuminates them with his meticulous draftsmanship and his keen sense of character and period.

Ding Cong is an all-round artist but above all a brilliant cartoonist and illustrator. A good illustration should do more than simply reproduce what a writer has said: it should give it a new dimension by adding the artist's insight. This Ding Cong does most successfully, using his cartoonist's eye to select significant details and bring out salient features without drawing caricatures. His illustrations in this book are not merely amusing but forceful and thought-provoking. Over the years he has evolved his distinctive style and simplified his compositions. His drawings can be recognized at a glance. The speed with which he now works is based on painstaking practice.

Ding Cong's old friends still call him Little Ding, not simply because he won fame under this name but because of his lovable childlike qualities. He is frank, enthusiastic and straightforward, full of fun and with no malice in his make-up. Wherever he goes we hear laughter. "The style is the man" this applies to both writers and artists.

Ding Cong now still advises the literary journal *Du Shu*. One of China's prolific artists, he is working tirelessly to delight the reading public.

**Gladys Yang
and
Yang Xianyi**

September 1992

# 丁聪和他的漫画

　　1985年丁聪曾出版过一本古代笑话插图集，内容是讽刺某些昏庸官僚和装模作样的愚蠢人物，表现了近两千年间中国人民古老的幽默。这本集子受到读者极大的欢迎，他们要求作者再画一本反映当今社会中存在的愚昧、不合理现象的讽刺作品，成为《古趣集》的姐妹篇——《今趣集》。

　　《古趣集》出版至今已7年，丁聪也已到了76岁高龄，他的身体仍然很健康，不断作画，画稿上依然署着"小丁"的笔名。他的父亲丁悚是过去上海的漫画家。丁聪在十几岁时就随父亲作画。因为家中经常有一些著名戏曲演员、作家和美术家来作客，因此他从小就喜爱艺术。当时的画家生活很艰苦；他的父亲并不想鼓励他成为画家，也不愿意教他画画；他开始只是把绘画当作业余爱好，作一些生活速写。后来也只在上海美专正规学习了一个学期。

　　与他同时代的大多数画家一样，丁聪经历过颠沛流离的生活。抗日战争迫使他离开上海去内地，后来由于国民党对文艺的审查制度和政治迫害，他被迫流亡到香港。解放后的反右运动和"文化大革命"又剥夺了他20年的创作自由，许多署自己名字的作品不能发表。即使这样，他还是创作了大量的作品，这确令人惊异。艰苦生活环境磨炼了他的意志，丰富了他的生活经验，也增加了他对过去受苦受难的老百姓的感情。

丁聪开始主要是创作漫画,同时也编辑过电影画报,从事美术编辑工作。在内地和香港期间还设计过舞台布景。这些经验对他为小说作插图很有帮助。太平洋战争爆发以后,他从香港回到内地参加"香港受难"展览,并随剧团到各地写生,接触到当时难民的生活,画出他们困苦的处境。如他在成都曾为当时妓女的悲惨生活画了一幅"花街",还画了其它揭露战时国民党腐败社会的作品。由于他的贡献,他成为当时中国美术家协会的一位杰出代表。

1944年,他为鲁迅的名著《阿Q正传》画了插图,讽刺了当时的地主阶级和假洋鬼子,对天真的阿Q的苦难遭遇表示了同情。他对贫苦大众的深厚感情都体现在他那个时期的作品之中。

1945年他回到上海,后来又去香港,在那个时期作了不少抨击国民党反动统治的漫画。他曾经说过:"漫画犹如匕首,可以用来刺穿那个黑暗悲惨的年代!"

解放后,他来到北京,编辑了《人民画报》,又画了不少漫画和书籍插图,设计过各种展览。五十年代初,在丁聪布置的一次古典小说《红楼梦》的展览会上,我们相识了。他笑咪咪地,象个弥勒佛,兴致勃勃地带着我们看他的那些美术设计。那次展览的大量资料提供了"红楼梦"一书的历史背景,当时的服装和生活用具,甚至包括宫廷科举制度下考场作弊的材料等等。那是我们所见过的一次最有趣味的展览。

1957年丁聪被错划为右派,到北大荒劳改。虽然有时气温低到零下30度,他毫无怨恨情绪,仍保持着自己的幽默。1960年他恢复名誉,到美术馆工作,但在1966年"文化大革命"期间又被送到干校,当上了猪倌。

1979年他恢复自由后，决定要补上所失掉的时间。请他作画的很多，他在许多报纸和刊物上发表漫画，并为不少著名作家如鲁迅、老舍和茅盾等人的小说画了插图。在认真研究这些作品之后，他精心绘制了插图，忠实地反映了作品内容、人物性格和时代特征。

丁聪是一位多才多艺、技巧全面的画家，特别擅长的是漫画和书籍插图。一幅好的插图不仅能反映出作家所说的内容，而且能加深作品的艺术深度。丁聪正是成功地做到了这一点。他以画家敏锐的洞察力选出重要的细节，取其精华，而不使人物漫画化。他为这本书所作的插图不仅使人觉得有趣，而且使人深思。他的独特风格和简洁手法是长期探索的果实。他作画速度惊人，画面简洁明了，而这正是他苦心经营的成绩。

丁聪的老朋友们都叫他"小丁"，这不仅是因为他年少成名，而且是因为他"不失其赤子之心"，为人坦率、真诚、正直。他到哪里，人们都会听到他那爽朗的笑声。他的作品的风格正反映了他本人的性格。

丁聪现在仍是《读书》杂志的美术顾问，还是中国美术家协会漫画艺术委员会主任。他不知疲倦，经常发表新作品，数量惊人。他常说，自己已到古稀之年了，必须加倍努力。

戴乃迭　杨宪益
*1992 年 9 月*

## 1. Leave Together

Wife: "This place is a wreck. I can't stand it anymore, I'm leaving."
Husband: "You're right. This place is a wreck. Wait, I'll go with you."

## 一 起 走

女:"这个家,我再也呆不下去了,我马上就离开……"
男:"这个家,我也呆不下去了,等等我,我和你一起走。"

## 2. Don't Always Arrive Late

Daughter: "Everytime I have a date with him, he never shaves. I just don't know why."
Father: "Maybe in the future you shouldn't arrive so late."

### 别老迟到

女儿:"我每次跟他约会,他下巴的胡子总是没刮干净,不知什么原因?"
父亲:"以后约会,你不要再迟到太久就行了。"

## 3. Wedding Wear

Bride: "Wasn't that suit just tailored for the wedding? How did it get so big? It doesn't even fit you."

Groom: "It's merely the result of runnning all over the place for the past several months trying to execute your wedding plans."

## 婚 服

新娘:"这套新衣服,不是为了结婚才量体新做的吗?怎么做得这么不合身?"

新郎:"这几个月来,为了满足你的结婚要求,天天东奔西跑的结果啊!"

## 4. So Thin

"I haven't seen you for several months, how did you get so thin?"
"I was transferred out of the kitchen."

## 瘦 的 原 因

"几个月不见,你怎么瘦了?"
"他们把我从厨房调出来了。"

## 5. The Mirror in the Exhibition Parlour

"The woman in this painting is, oh, so ugly."
"I wouldn't complain if I were you, my dear. That's no painting, it's a mirror."

## 展厅里的镜子

"这幅画里的女人丑死了!"
"别嚷嚷,你看的是一面镜子。"

## 6. Pulse

"Your pulse is pretty normal. Every minute it beats exactly sixty times."

## 脉　搏

"脉搏还可以嘛,每分钟六十跳……"

## 7. The Wife's Not Home

"Ha ha, you may have made off with the fish, but let's see you eat it without the recipe!"

## 妻子不在家

"哈哈,你抢得了鱼,可烹饪法在我手里,看你怎么吃!?"

## 8. Imported Watch

"Hey, how come your watch is off by a few hours?"
"This watch is imported. It's still on foreign time."

### 进 口 时 间

"你的表怎么差几个小时?"
"我的表是进口的,走的是进口时间。"

## 9. True Gentleman

"Your house caught fire and burned down!"
"Why didn't you mention it earlier?!"
"I am a true gentleman, I didn't want to disrupt the game."

## "真 君 子"

"你家着火,把房子都烧掉啦!"

"你怎么不早说?"

"我是'观棋不语的真君子'。"

## 10. Theatrical Performance

Actress: "Today's performance was unexpectedly well-received. I went out three times to take a bow and the audience went wild with applause."
Director: "Of course, they did. Your fake nose is falling off."

### 剧场效果

演员:"今天的剧场效果出人意外,我谢幕三次,观众还掌声如雷……"

导演:"那是自然的,因为你把假鼻子弄歪了。"

## 11. The Honorarium

A doctor submitted an article on the hazzards of smoking. After receiving his honorarium in the mail, the doctor's son asked, "Dad, how much did you get?"

The father replied, "Two cartons of Marlboro."

## 稿　酬

某医生发表了讲吸烟危害性的文章。稿酬寄来后,儿子问:"爸爸,多少钱?"

爸爸说:"两条'万宝路'。"

## 12. World Record

A champion athelete caught a serious flu and lay resting in bed unable to get up. When the doctor told him he had a fever he asked, "Doctor, what's my temperature?"

The doctor replied, "41 degrees Celsius."

The athelete then quickly inquired, "By the way, what's the world record temperature?"

## 世界纪录

冠军运动员因患重感冒卧床不起,医生告诉他发烧了。他问道:"体温多少度?"答:"四十一度。"

运动员忙又问:"那么世界纪录是多少?"

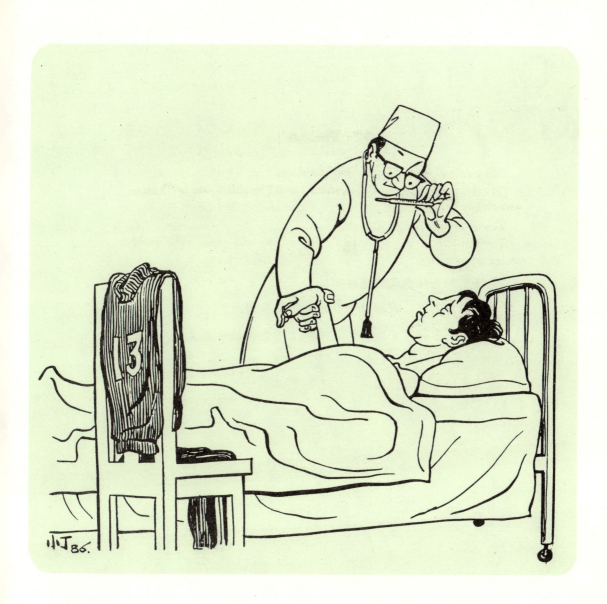

## 13. Vision

"Why do you wear glasses when you sleep?"
"My vision isn't very good. I'm afraid I won't be able to see my dreams very clearly."

### 视　　力

"你睡觉时为什么还戴眼镜？"
"我的视力不佳，我担心做梦时看不清东西。"

## 14. Three Idiots

Father: "Tell me, what's one plus three?"
Son: "I don't know."
Father: "For example, you, your mother and I altogether are how many, you idiot?!"
Son: "Three idiots."

## 三个笨蛋

父亲:"你说,一加二等于几?"

儿子:"不知道。"

父亲:"譬如说,我跟你妈妈,再加上你,一共等于几?笨蛋!"

儿子:"三个笨蛋。"

## 15. I Laughed Last Year

"Look, this cartoon is absolutely ridiculous, how can you have no reaction."

"I already laughed last year."

## 我去年笑过了

甲:"瞧,这幅漫画太可笑了,你怎么毫无反应?"
乙:"我在去年早已笑过了。"

## 16. Not Completely Copied

Teacher: "How come you completely copied somebody else's homework?"
Student: "I didn't completely copy it. My name is different."

### 不是全抄

老师:"你的作业,怎么全是抄别人的?!"
学生:"不是全抄,我的名字没有抄。"

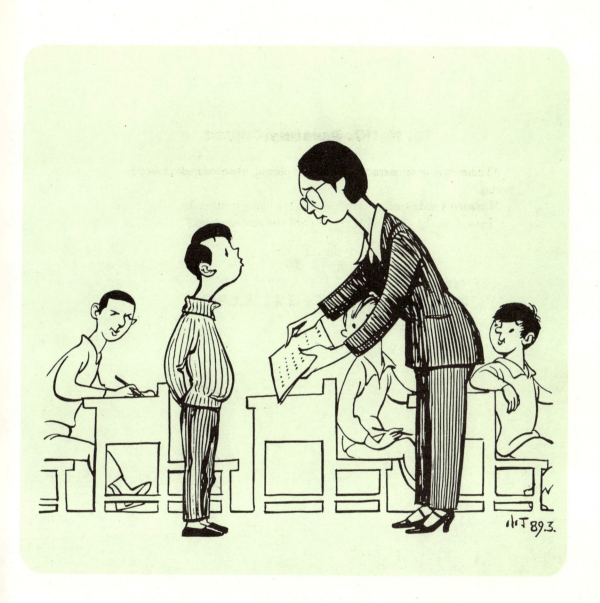

## 17. Boredom

"Those two guys were up all night playing their stupid chess. So boring!"
"How do you know?"
"I stood on the side and watched until the sun came up."

## 无　聊

甲:"他俩的臭棋,昨晚竟下了个通宵,太无聊了!"
乙:"你怎么知道的?"
甲:"我在旁边一直看到天亮。"

## 18. Throw Out the Cat

Wife: "How come this awful cat is still here? Didn't I tell you to take him to a faraway place and throw him away?!"

Husband: "I took him out to a desolate place far from town, but ... without the cat I couldn't find my way home."

### 扔 猫

妻子:"怎么这讨厌的猫还在,我叫你跑远点去扔么!"

丈夫:"我跑到老远的荒郊野外,可是……要没有它,我几乎找不到家了。"

## 19. Teacher Is Not as Good as I Am

Son: "Mom, my teacher Mrs. Zhang's Chinese isn't as good as mine."
Mother: "Don't be ridiculous."
Son: "No, it's true. I can recognize the characters that she writes, but she cannot recognize mine."

### 老师不如我

儿子:"妈妈,张老师的语文不如我。"

妈妈:"你胡说!"

儿子:"真的嘛,她写的字我认得,我写的字,她还不认识呢!"

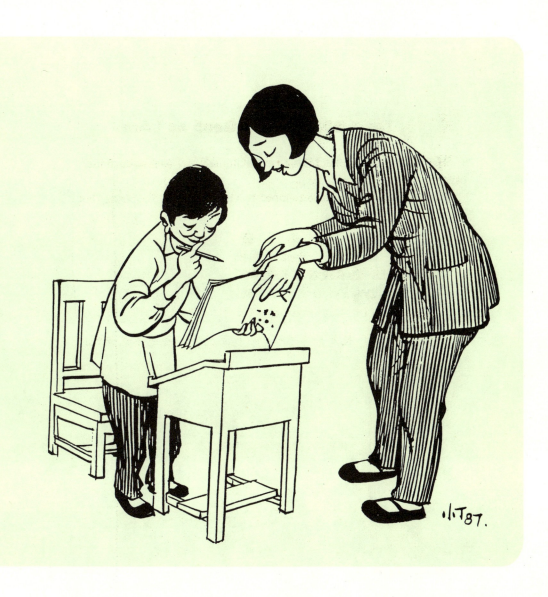

## 20. Stamp a Seal

"How come your father didn't stamp his seal on your examination paper?"
"He did it all right, but he stamped it here."

### 盖　章

"你的试卷上，怎么没有家长盖章？"

"盖啦，盖在这里。"

## 21. Alterations

"Look at this shirt you tailored for me. The collar is too small and the sleeve too long."

"Don't worry about it. The collar will get bigger as you wear it and the sleeve will shrink after you wash it a couple times."

## 没 关 系

"你替我做的衬衫，领子太小了，袖子太长了……"

"没关系，领子穿穿会大的，袖子洗洗会缩短的。"

## 22. Observations

A father told his son of his first experience abroad: "The people had an incredibly high level of culture. Even young children could speak the 'foreign' language!"

### 考察的体会

父亲对儿子说初次出国"考察"的体会。
"人家的文化水平就是高，连小孩子都会讲外语。"

## 23. Five-Step Snake

While on an excursion, a father turned to his son and said, "'Be very careful. In these parts there is a kind of snake called the 'five-step snake.' If it bites you, you will die after walking only five steps."

The son replied, "It doesn't matter, if I get bitten by the snake I'll stop walking after four steps."

"If you do it that way, you will be only one step away from death. It would be much more safe not to take the first step at all."

## 五 步 蛇

父子俩去郊游，父亲对儿子说："要小心啊，此处有种蛇叫'五步蛇'，被它咬伤，走五步就死。"

"没关系，万一被五步蛇咬了，我只走四步就不再走了。"

"你那样做，离死只差一步了；一步也不要走才最保险。"

## 24. Giving Fish

"Mr. Section Chief, I brought over several big fish for you."
"Ai-ya, now is a period of rectification in the Party, I can by no means accept any favours."
"Well, then I'll just give them to your wife instead."
"This I have no objection to. She's one of the masses."

送 鱼

"科长,我给你送来了几条又大又肥的鱼。"
"哎呀,现在是整党整风,这鱼我可不能收。"
"那就送给您夫人吧?"
"这我就不管了,反正她是群众。"

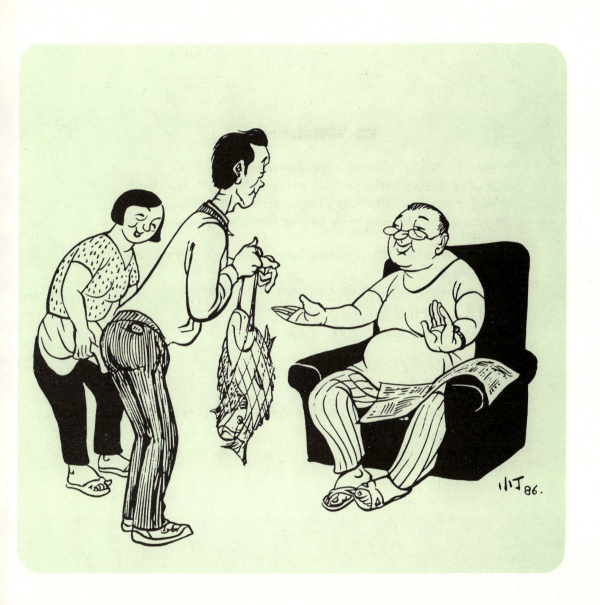

## 25. Efficiency

Factory manager: "Have the newspapers come yet?"
Head of mailroom: "Not yet."
Factory manager: "What's up with the postal system anyway. With this type of poor efficiency, when will the 'Four Modernizations' ever be realized?"
Head of mailroom: "Don't worry about it, maybe the papers will come this afternoon."
Factory manager: "Now what am I going to do this morning."

## 效 率

厂长:"报纸来了没有?"
收发:"还没有。"
厂长:"邮电局怎么搞的,象这样的效率,'四化'什么时候能实现?"
收发:"您别急,可能下午来。"
厂长:"那我上午干什么?"

## 26. After Losing the Cat

The bureau head's family lost their beloved cat. Some of the other cadres pooled together some money to buy them a new one. Sighing, the bureau head's wife said, "Ohhh, if only we had told them we lost a colour television instead...."

## 丢猫以后

局长家丢了一只心爱的猫。

赵科长、钱股长、孙组长……纷纷前来送猫。

局长夫人惋惜地说:"要是告诉他们,我家丢了一台彩色电视机该多好。"

## 27. Persistence

"I'm not feeling very well. Tonight I won't attend a leadership conference."

"The leadership conference was moved to tomorrow night, instead a movie will be shown tonight."

"In that case, give me the ticket, I'll make the effort to watch it."

## 贵在坚持

"我身体不舒服,今晚我不参加领导班子会议了。"

"领导班子会议改在明天晚上开了,今晚上映内部电影。"

"那戏票还是给我,我再坚持一下看看。"

## 28. New Law to Protect Forests

Forest ranger: "There are always people who seek to damage the trees."

County magistrate: "Well, you could put up a sign on all of the trees, warning, 'Damaging Trees Is Prohibited.'"

Forest ranger: "With the wind and the rain, in only a few short days the signs will fall off."

County magistrate: "Then carve the notice into the trees themselves."

## 护 林 新 法

护林员:"总有人损坏树木。"

县　　长:"那就在每棵树上贴张纸条:'不许损坏树木!'"

护林员:"风吹雨淋,几天就掉了。"

县　　长:"那就刻在树上吧!"

67

## 29. Installing the Doorbell

The section chief moved into a new house. Strangely enough, he asked the electrician to install the doorbell at the bottom of the doorshaft.

Thinking this request somewhat peculiar, the electrician asked, "How will guests ring the doorbell?"

The section chief replied, "My guests all use their foot to ring the doorbell because their hands are always full of gifts for me."

### 装 门 铃

张科长搬进新居,要电工在门下侧装一个电铃按钮。

电工奇怪地问:"这叫来客怎么按呢?"

张科长回答:"我的客人都是用脚踢门,因为手里已经拿满礼物了。"

## 30. Steps to Reform

"Sir, what steps do you plan to take in reforming the dining hall."
"The old method: no price ceiling, no quality guarantees."

## 改革的措施

"师傅,你对食堂的改革,有什么具体措施?"
"老办法:价格不封顶,质量不保证。"

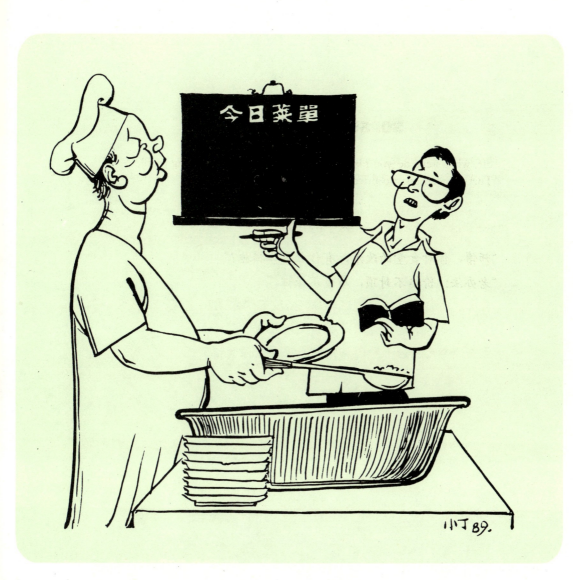

## 31. Dealing with Complaints

Worker: "About the issue of lowering the temperature in our workshop, we've already raised many complaints. Have they just been thrown away on the scrap heap, or what?"

Supervisor: "What kind of talk is that? These complaints have all been stored intact in the file cabinet."

## 意见的处理

工人:"我们对车间的降温问题,提过不少意见和建议,可一直没有下文,是不是都当废纸处理了?"

主任:"哪儿的话,它们都完好地保存在档案柜里呢。"

## 32. Solving the Problem of Meetings and Documents

"From the reaction of the cadres and the masses, we hold too many meetings and circulate too many documents. Do you think we can cut down on these practices?"

"Okay, we can immediately hold a meeting to discuss this issue and pass out the decision afterward."

### 解决"文山会海"法

"现在干部、群众反映：会议、文件太多，是否可以想办法少开少发一些？"

"好啊，我们马上开会研究一下，把决定发个文件下去。"

## 33. Habits Become the Norm

After finishing reading her son's letter, the woman handed it to her dozing husband. The man glanced at it for a moment and then jotted down the word "approved."

The woman laughed, "What? Are you crazy?"

The man patted his brow and said, "Oh, I forgot I'm at home."

## 习惯成自然

太太看完儿子的信,递给正在闭目养神的丈夫。老头儿瞟了一眼,就批了"同意"二字。

太太笑道:"你疯啦?"

老头儿一扬脑门儿:"哟,我忘了是在家里了。"

## 34. No Vacancies—Vacancies

"Excuse me, do you have any rooms?"

"No. Didn't you see the sign?"

"The Manager of the Hotel Service Department is coming to hold a conference. He'll be here in just a moment."

"Why didn't you mention it earlier? How many rooms do you need?"

### 无房——有房

"请问，还有床位吗？"

"没有，你没看见?!"

"是服务公司经理要来开个会，等一下小车就到。"

"哎，你怎么不早说！要几间？"

## 35. The Friends of the Head of Department X

"I heard that you have many good friends. May I ask, how many do you actually have?"

"I can't really say for sure at this time. Wait until next month after I retire then I can really tell you."

## ×长的朋友

"听说你有许多好朋友,请问到底有多少位?"

"现在说不准,等下个月我离退下来后,就可以告诉你了。"

## 36. Go to Work

"Mom, you guys are having another meeting at work today, huh?!"

## 上 班 去

"妈妈,今天大概又是要开会听报告吧?!"

## 37. Clap Your Hands

"This lecture is horrible. How can you applaud like that?"
"I'm just happy it's finally over!"

### 鼓　掌

"又臭又长的报告，你还给他鼓掌？"

"他总算讲完了！"

## 38. Goods Coming at the Same Time

"This fish isn't as fresh as the one that I bought last week!"
"Don't be ridiculous. This fish is exactly as fresh as that one. They both came into the store at the same time."

## 同时进的货

"这鱼不如我上星期买的新鲜!"

"胡说,这鱼和那鱼一样新鲜,是同时进的货。"

## 39. Conserve Electricity, Buy Glasses

"You may be conserving electricity, but you'll ruin your eyes!"
"I'm only conserving electricity so I can afford to buy glasses."

### 省电买眼镜

"你节省电费,可是看坏了眼睛!"
"我就是为了配眼镜才节省电费的。"

## 40. Misunderstanding

"What are you doing cutting up the picture album I just bought?"
"Oops! I thought you borrowed it from the library."

误　会

"你怎么裁我刚买回的画册?"

"槽糕! 我以为你是从图书馆借来的呢。"

## 41. Choose Your Own Height

"Now I can say I'm of average height!"

### 选择你的标准身高

"现在,我的身高够标准了吧!"

## 42. The Worried Husband

"This time I didn't forget to bring my umbrella home."
"But, you didn't take *your* umbrella out today."

### 粗心的丈夫

"这回我可没忘记把雨伞带回来。"
"可你今天没有带伞出去呀!"

## 43. Family Law

"Our teacher said that a father hitting his child is against the law."
"Idiot! Your teacher was talking about the national law. This falls under family law."

### "家　　法"

"老师说，爸爸打儿子也是犯法的。"
"笨蛋！老师说的是国法，我打你用的是家法。"

## 44. Visit the Home

A teacher went to visit his student's home. Upon entering the door he noticed that his student was smoking a cigarette. Both teacher and student stood there bewildered, not knowing what to say.

Just then the student's father appeared and immediately began to reproach his child, "What's wrong with you! How come you didn't offer a cigarette to your teacher?"

## 家 访

老师去家访，一进门看见他的学生正在抽烟，师生二人一时都楞住了。

家长一见，忙责备孩子："光知道自个儿抽，还不快给老师点上一支。"

## 45. Taking a Break

"After work I have to line up to buy food, help my kid with his homework, do the wash, and even do some carpentry...."
"When do you have a chance to take a break?"
"When I'm at work."

## 休息的时候

"下班后,我要排队买菜,要给孩子补功课,要洗衣服,还要做木工活……"
"那你什么时候休息呢?"
"上班的时候。"

## 46. The Difference Between Inside and Out

"Mom, it's just like you said. He wants to take care of *his* mother, so I broke up with him."

"Shhh ... don't be so loud. The people in the inner room will hear you."

"Who's in the inner room?"

"Your younger brother and his girlfriend."

### 内 外 有 别

"妈,就照你说的,他要养他妈,我就跟他吹!"

"嘘——小声点,别让里屋听见。"

"里屋有谁呀?"

"你二弟和他的对象。"

## 47. The Art of Hypnosis

"It's already very late and our son's not willing to go to sleep. Could you read him one of your reports?"

"How is a little child like him going to understand a 'report.'"

"Since your reports are so boring, after listening for a couple of minutes he'll be sound asleep."

## 催 眠 新 术

"宝宝深更半夜还不肯睡觉,求求你起来给他做个报告。"

"小孩子怎么听得懂报告?"

"因为你的报告有催眠作用。只要你一做报告,听的人就睡着了。"

## 48. Worried

"The manager transferred Little Li to the hardware department. I'm really worried about her."

"What are you worried about?"

"When Little Li was in the food department she would eat anything she sold. I'm just worried that in the hardware department she end up chipping some teeth."

## 担　心

"经理把小李调到五金组,我真替小李担心。"

"担心什么?"

"小李在食品组的时候,卖什么吃什么。这一下调到五金组我真担心她碰坏了牙齿。"

## 49. Scenes at the Hospital

Patient: "How can a sick person possibly eat this awful food?"
Attendant: "Did you come here to eat food or did you come here to eat medicine?"

## 某医院见闻

住院病号:"这样低劣的饭菜,病人怎么能吃呢?"

医院服务员:"你是来吃药的? 还是来吃饭的?"

## 50. Think of a Way

"Your wife has had a toothache for two days already. Why don't you think of a way to deal with this problem?"

"I thought of it! I stick cotton in my ears."

### 想 办 法

"你妻子牙痛已有两天了,你为什么不替她想想办法?"

"我想了呀!我在耳朵里塞了块棉花。"

## 51. Overlooked

Customer: "How come the drinks you sell here taste so watered down?"
Waiter (after tasting the wine): "Sorry, I forgot to mix in the alcohol."

## 疏　　忽

顾客:"你们卖的酒怎么没酒味呀?"

服务员接过一闻:"对不起,我忘了给你掺酒了。"

## 52. Misfortune

Mother: "Aren't you preparing to register to get married?"
Daughter: "Oh, I don't even bring it up. I've really been unfortunate."
Mother: "Has that man deceived you?"
Daughter: "No, it's just that his father, the influential cadre, just passed away."

### 不　　幸

母亲:"你不是准备登记结婚吗?"

女儿:"咳，别提了，我真不幸。"

母亲:"是那个小伙子欺骗了你?"

女儿:"不，是他的局长爸爸死了。"

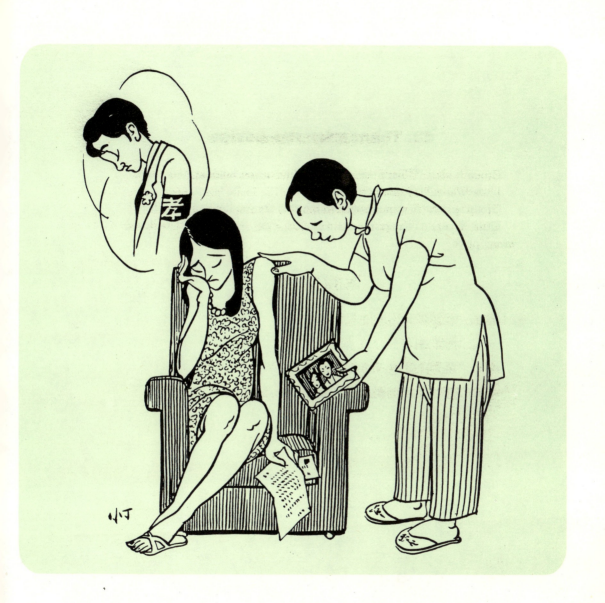

## 53. Thanks for the Advice

Group leader: "What's the matter? Why are you holding your chest?"
Little Wang: "My stomach aches."
Group leader: "If your stomach hurts, why are you holding your chest?"
Little Wang: "Thanks for your advice. Next time I won't hold the wrong place."

## 谢 谢 指 教

组长:"你怎么啦?总捂着胸口?"

小王:"我胃痛。"

组长:"胃是在腹部,你怎么捂着胸口?"

小王:"谢谢你的指教,下次我就不会捂错了。"

## 54. Giving Out Bonus Money

Master: "You just have your bonus, how can you be sitting here like a bump on a log?"
Apprentice: "Whether I work or not, I still have the bonus."

### 发 奖 金

师傅:"怎么发了奖金你还不干活呢?"
徒弟:"因为不干活也照样发奖金。"

## 55. Photos

Customer: "What! How did I get to look like that?!"
Photographer (coldly): "A person's picture comes out the way he looks."
Customer (suddenly understanding): "Oh, so you mean to say that I look very blurry."

## 照　像

顾客:"怎么？我怎么成了这个样子？"
照像师（冷漠地）:"人长得什么样，照出来就是什么样。"
顾客（恍然大悟地）:"哦，原来我长得模糊。"

## 56. Measuring Height

"Little boy, let me measure you."
"My mom already measured me."
"How tall?"
"I'm free of charge under one metre in the bus; I'm admitted just over one metre into a movie house."

### 量 身 高

"小朋友,给你量一量身高。"
"妈妈给我量过了。"
"多少?"
"坐汽车是二尺九,上影院是三尺一。"

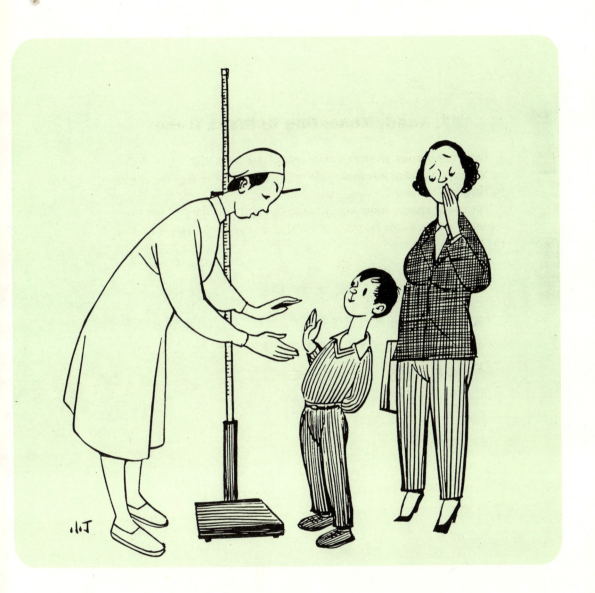

## 57. Ready-Made Pits to Plant Trees

"How come every year your work unit plants trees here?"

"Last year we dug pits here. This year we can save energy digging up the loosened ground."

"So where are the trees you planted last year?"

"They were already recorded as planted quotas in the report back to the higher authorities."

现 坑 种 树

"你们单位怎么年年在这里种树?"

"去年我们在这里挖过坑,今年挖起来省力呀!"

"那去年种的树呢?"

"已经写进给上级的汇报材料里去了。"

## 58. Still Effective

"This article in the paper says that the medicine you prescribed for me is no longer good."

"Don't worry about it. Since you contracted this ailment before this article was published, the medicine is still good for you."

## 仍 然 有 效

"您给我开的药,昨天报上已经公布停止使用了。"

"不要紧,您的病是在公布以前得的,所以这药对您仍然有效。"

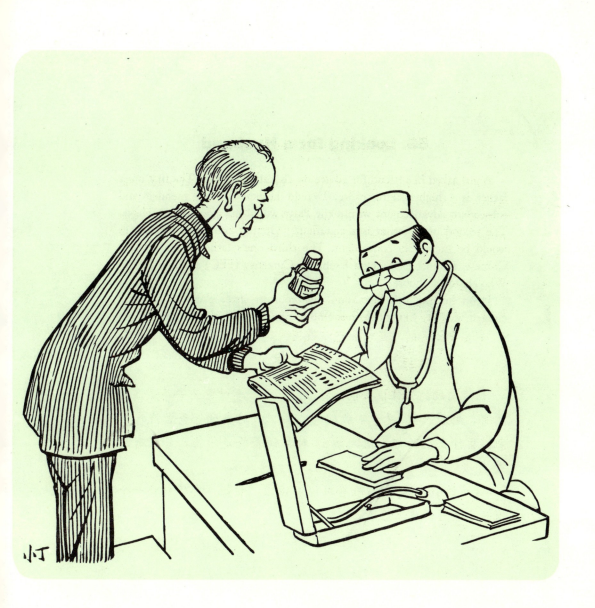

## 59. Looking for a Husband

A girl asked her friend for advice on choosing a mate: "The first one's father is a high-ranking cadre. I could become a Party member and subsequent advancement within the Party would not pose any problems. The second one's father is a chauffeur. Getting around to buy things would be incredibly convenient. The third one's father is an overseas Chinese. I could get Foreign Exchange Currency (FEC) anytime I wish. Who should I choose?"

Upon hearing this discussion, her younger sister glared at her and chimed in, "Sis, you should just find a man who has three fathers."

## 找 对 象

姑娘向她的女伴说择偶的标准:"第一，要对象的爸爸是高级干部，婚后入党、提干不成问题；第二，对象的爸爸是汽车司机，买什么东西都方便；第三，对象的爸爸是华侨，外汇有的是。"

姑娘的小妹妹听见，瞪着眼望着姐姐:"姐姐，那你就找一个有三个爸爸的对象好了。"

## 60. Know Whom to Lie to

A father gave his son a few whacks with a bamboo stick and said, "Are you still going to lie to me?"
The son sadly replied, "I won't tell any more lies!"
"Now, from this day on what should you do?"
"I'll just do what you do, only tell lies to Mom."

## 看对象撒谎

父亲扬起手中的竹板,打一下儿子问一声:"你还跟我说谎不?"儿子哀告道:"不撒谎啦!"

"那么,今后该怎么做?"

"跟爸爸一样,只对妈妈撒谎。"

## 61. Stay Out of Other's Business

Son: "Dad, somebody's wallet is being pickpocketed."
Father: "That's none of your business."
Son: "But it's yours."
Father: "Ahh!!!...."

少 管 闲 事

儿子:"爸爸,小偷摸钱包啦!"

父亲:"你少管闲事。"

儿子:"是偷您的!"

父亲:"啊! ……"

## 62. All Different Kinds

"I see the rice in your restaurant comes in all different varieties."
"What? We only serve one kind."
"No, you have raw, cooked, and half-raw/half-cooked."

### 花样繁多

"你们饭馆的米饭真是花样繁多。"

"不就一种吗?"

"不,有生的,有熟的,还有半生不熟的。"

## 63. Not Always

"How come the umbrellas that your factory puts out always leak?"
"Don't exaggerate. They don't always leak, only when it rains."

### 并非老是

"你们厂生产的雨伞怎么老是漏水呀?"
"别夸张说'老是',只有雨天才漏水呗。"

## 64. Lingering Fear

Upon seeing his wife's factory's security section chief appear at the door, the husband quickly took the things his wife had brought home earlier that day and stuffed them in the drawers and underneath the bureau.

Laughing, his wife asked, "What the heck are you doing?"

The husband replied in a whisper, "I was worried you brought these things home from the factory."

## 心 有 余 悸

丈夫看见妻子厂里的保卫科长出现在门口,急忙把妻子今天带回来的东西往抽屉里、桌子下乱塞。

妻子见了笑道:"你这是干什么呀?"

丈夫低声说:"我怕你这些东西,又是从厂里拿回来的。"

## 65. Father and Son

Father: "Son, if you don't pass the college entrance exam, I will disown you."

Son: "Dad, if do I pass the college entrance exam, I will disown *you*."

### 父 与 子

"孩子,你要是考不进大学,我就不认你这个儿子。"

"爸爸,我要是考进了大学,我就不认你这个爸爸。"

## 66. No Future

"She is a janitor who cleans the restrooms. She sacrifices her cleanliness so that everyone else will have clean facilities. Look, her picture was even put in the paper. What an honour."
"Dad, when I grow up I want to be a janitor."
"Don't be ridiculous. You'll never make anything out of yourself!"

### 没 出 息

"她是一个清洁工,为大家扫厕所,一人脏换来万人净,报上还有她的照片呐!多光荣。"
"爸爸,我长大了也当清洁工。"
"胡说,你这孩子真没出息!"

## 67. After Marriage

Wife: "In the past, you were always gentle and caring, now you just sit around and make faces."
Husband: "In the past, we had not yet gotten married."

## 婚　后

女:"你过去对我总是十分温柔、体贴,现在怎么变成这付嘴脸?!"
男:"那时候我们还没有结婚。"

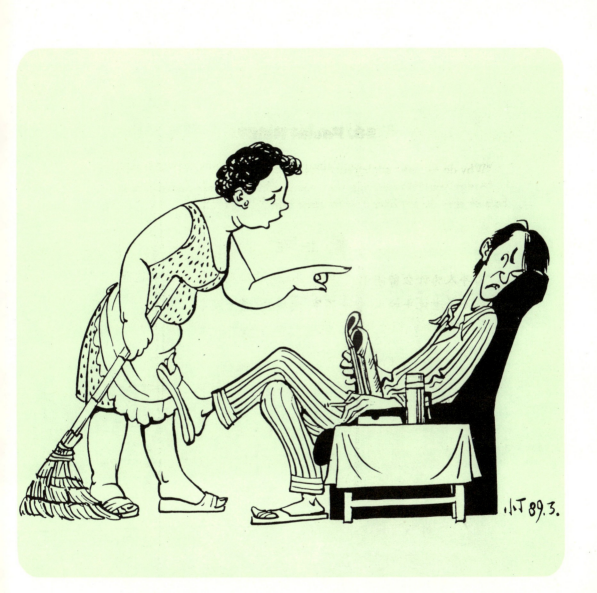

## 68. Facial Hair

"Why do so many adolescents grow beards?"
"Aren't you always saying that young adolescents are undependable because they do not have hair on their faces."

## 嘴 上 毛

"青年人为什么留胡子？"
"你不是老说年轻人'办事不牢'是因为'嘴上没毛'么！"

## 69. Washing Machine

"How come I haven't seen your mom around here for the last two days?"

"I asked her to leave."

"Leave? Didn't you say you were going to let her live here a couple more days?"

"Yes, but we just bought a washing machine."

## 洗 衣 机

"最近这两天,怎么看不到你妈妈?"

"给我打发走了。"

"走了?你不是说让她在你这儿多住几天吗?"

"我家买了洗衣机了。"

## 70. Deciphering a Love Letter

"Could you please help me read this letter from my boyfriend? There are a lot of words I cannot figure out. He's a doctor and...."

### "详"情书

"请帮我看看这封信,是我的男朋友写来的。许多字我不认识,他是当医生的。……"

## 71. Flies

"Hey, my food has a fly in it!"
"Huh? How could that be? I thought I picked out all of the flies before I brought the dish over here."

## 苍　蝇

"这盘菜里有只苍蝇!"
"咦?怎么搞的?我端上来之前,已经把苍蝇都拣出来了。"

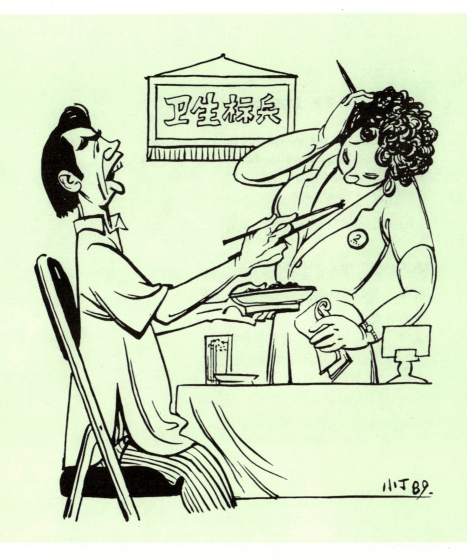

## 72. Doctor's Orders

"While you're sick you should only consume liquids."
"Great! Normally my favourite thing to do is to drink liquids."
"What kind of liquids?"
"Booze!"

## 医　　嘱

"患病期间，你只能吃流质。"

"好极了，平时我最喜欢吃的就是流质。"

"什么流质？"

"酒！"

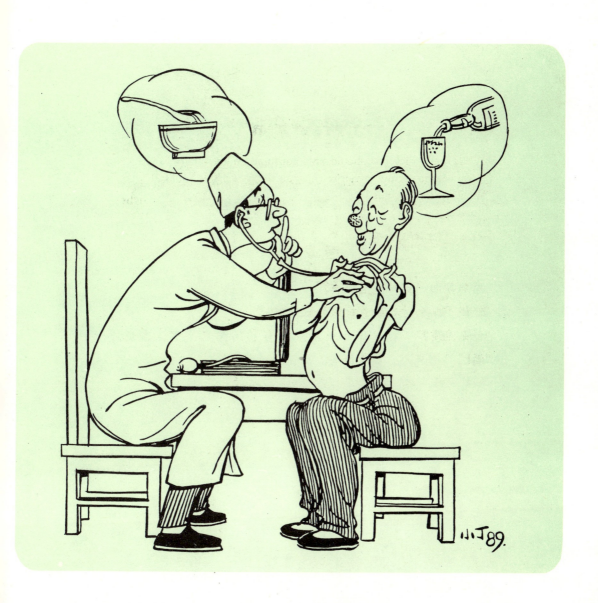

## 73. "Yes" Man

Son: "Mom, what is a 'yes' man?"
Mother: "Umm—it's a person who never gives his own opinion about anything, always agreeing with what has been said. Isn't that right, honey?"
Father: "Yes, yes, yes!"

## 唯唯诺诺的人

儿子:"妈妈,什么叫做唯唯诺诺的人?"

妈妈:"唔——就是那些从不发表自己的意见,嘴上常说'对、对、对'的人。孩子他爸,我说得对吗?"

爸爸:"对、对、对!"

## 74. Looking Like a Scholar

An uneducated young man began walking around with a fountain pen inserted in his shirt pocket. Many people assumed he was a man of some knowledge. The young man was tickled pink, and decided to insert a second fountain pen in his shirt pocket. Before long, people began to comment, "This guy must be a college student or an editor." Upon overhearing this, the young man became even happier. He immediately added three more fountain pens. Afterwards, people started to gaze at him with looks of confusion, some saying, "He probably just works in a pen repair shop."

## 显示学问

某青年不学无术，却常在衣兜里插一支钢笔。别人以为他有点学问，他听了很高兴，就在衣兜里又插上一支。有人议论："此人不是个大学生，就是个编辑。"他听了更高兴了，在衣兜里一下插了五支钢笔。见到他的人都以惊疑不解的目光看着他。有人议论："大概是个修钢笔的吧！"

## 75. Whoever Returns Home First

"What are you doing here a block away from your house pacing back and forth? How come you don't just go home?"

"My wife said to me whoever gets home first makes dinner."

"Ahh, no wonder I just saw your wife pacing back and forth about a block away from your house in the other direction."

### 谁先回到家

"你怎么还不回家,老在家门附近来回转?"

"我和妻子说好了,谁先到家谁做饭。"

"怪不得,我刚才在路那边,看到你的妻子也在来回转呢!"

## 76. High and Low Voices

"Can you explain to me what the difference is between a high-pitched and low-pitched voice?"

"A high-pitched voice is when my father scolds me; a low-pitched voice is when my father speaks with his boss."

## 高 低 音

"你能解释什么是男高音？什么是男低音吗？"

"我爸爸训我的时候是男高音；爸爸见他上级说话时是男低音。"

## 77. Heroes Meet

"My boyfriend would like to meet you, Dad."

"What does he do for a living? How much money does he make a month?"

"Hmm, very interesting ... he asked the same questions about you."

### 英 雄 所 见

"我的男朋友想见见你,爸爸。"

"这小伙子干什么工作,一个月能挣多少钱?"

"这太有趣了,他也是这样问起您的!"

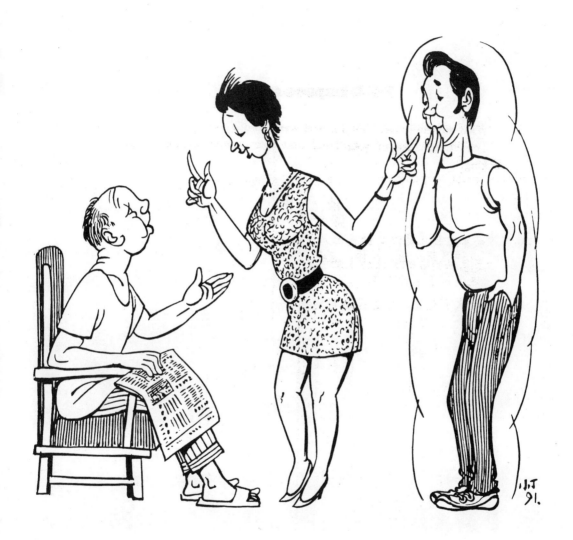

## 78. Disappearance

"What are the easiest things in the world to disappear?"
"The lit cigarette in your hand and your written pledge to quit smoking."

### 消　失

"世界上最容易消失的东西是什么?"
"是您抽的香烟和您的戒烟誓言。"

## 79. Mistaken

"What are you doing using the mosquito net over our bed to wipe off your shoes?"
"Ai-ya! I must be in a daze. I thought we were in a hotel!"

## 弄 错 了

"你怎么用我们床上的蚊帐擦皮鞋?"
"啊呀!我睡昏了,我还以为是在旅社呢!"

## 80. Way to Conserve Electricity

"How does your family pay so little on electricity?"
"We have early supper, and afterwards we go to a different neighbour's house to watch television. When we're finished, we go home to sleep. Every day we only need to turn on the lamp for a little while."

节 电 法

"你家用电怎么那么省?"
"每晚提早吃饭。饭后就轮流到宿舍区的邻居家看电视。看完回家就睡觉,只要开一会儿电灯就够啦。"

## 81. Applying for Welfare

"What happened to you? You look like a mess."
"I'm going down to apply for welfare subsidies. Do you think I look qualified enough?"

### 申请生活补助

"你怎么穿成这付狼狈相?"
"我正在申请生活补助,你看这身打扮合格吗。"

## 82. Wrong Place

"I wanted to reach for my handkerchief, but accidentally put my hand into your pocket. Sorry about that."

"I wanted to slap the mosquito on my face, but accidentally slapped you on the face. I'm sorry, too."

## 错 位

"我伸手掏我的手帕,掏错了你的口袋,抱歉!"

"我想打叮我脸上的蚊子,错打了你的耳光,对不起。"

## 83. Division of Labour

The boss turned to his secretary and said, "You lead the tour group. I'm too busy right now, so I'll only show up later at the banquet reception and eat with them."

分　工

领导对秘书说:"你带着观光团去参观吧。我因为工作太忙,只能出席招待宴会,陪他们吃顿饭。"

## 84. Air of a Leader

Director: "Where did you put the red pencil I correct documents with?"
Secretary: "The pencil is sitting behind your ear."
Director: "Quick, tell me which ear?"

## 领导的气派

主任:"你把我批文件的红铅笔搁哪儿去啦?"

秘书:"铅笔夹在您自己的耳朵上。"

主任:"哪只耳朵?快说!"

## 85. Confused Father

Wife: "What are you doing bringing somebody else's child home?"
Husband: "What's the difference? Anyway, early Monday morning I'll just take him back to the nursery school."

## 胡涂爸爸

妻子:"你怎么把别家的孩子接回来了?"
丈夫:"没关系,反正星期一早晨就把他送回托儿所的。"

## 86. Unwilling to Be Heartbroken

Wife: "As the saying goes, 'Smoking harms the lungs, drinking harms the liver.' You should quit them both!"
Husband: "If you don't let me smoke and drink it will break my heart. My heart is definitely more important than either my lungs or liver."

### 不愿伤"心"

妻子:"常言说:抽烟伤肺,喝酒伤肝,你把它们都戒了吧!"
丈夫:"不让我抽烟喝酒,我要伤心。心比肺和肝更要紧。"

## 87. Exchange of Experiences

Bricklayer: "Could your factory please give my factory the technology you use to produce those rock-hard cakes you make?"

Baker: "Could your factory please give my factory the technology you use to produce those limp, soft bricks you make?"

### 经 验 交 流

砖厂:"请你厂把如何能将糕点做得如此坚硬的技术传授给我厂。"

糕厂:"请你厂把如何能将砖头烧得如此酥松的技术传授给我厂。"

## 88. The Old Man Gives Up His Seat

"Please sit down, Miss."
"You're getting off soon?"
"No, but your popsicle is dripping all over the inside of my collar!"

## 老大爷让座

"姑娘,你请坐吧。"
"老大爷,您到站了吗?"
"不,你吃的冰棍水都滴在我脖子里!"

## 89. Old Legend, New Interpretation

"Why did Heavenly Queen want to break off the Cowherd Boy and the Girl Weaver's wedding?"
"Because the Cowherd Boy only had a rural residence permit."

### 旧俗新解

"王母娘娘干吗非要拆散牛郎织女的婚姻?"
"因为牛郎是农村户口。"

## 90. Each Has His Own Gains

"Mr. Director, this is the diploma from the correspondence college I took your tests for."

"Very good. I've acquired college level status and you've increased your knowledge."

### 各有所获

"这是我代替您读的函授大学的文凭,主任。"

"很好,我收到了'学历',你增长了知识。"

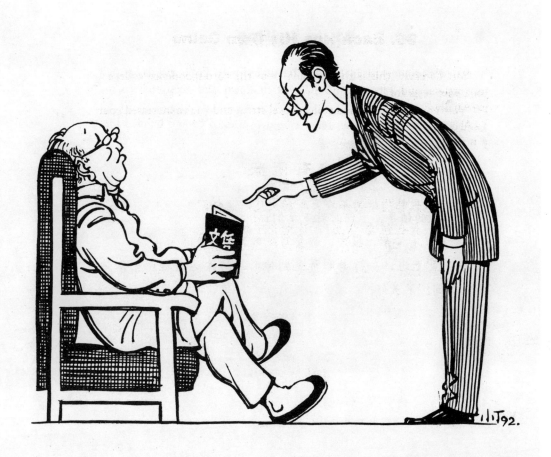

## 91. In Writing

A newly promoted leader said to his underlings, "From this day on, all instructions and reports must be written down and submitted to me personally."

At work the next day, an older employee walked by and handed him a note reading: "Good morning."

## 书　面

新提拔的领导，上任时对下属们说：
"今后凡有请示、报告，都要写成书面交给我。"
第二天上班，一位老职员见到他时，边走边交给他一张纸条，上写："早晨好。"

## 92. Incognito Inspection

An official went on a personal inspection of a factory's dining hall incognito. He asked one of the workers who was in the line to buy food, "How well is the dining hall run? Are you satisfied?"

"Are you asking about *today's* food or the usual grub?"

## "微服"私访

某领导到某工厂的食堂"微服"私访。他问买饭的工人:"你们厂的食堂办得怎么样?满意不满意?"

"您问的是今天的伙食?还是平时的?"

## 93. Egg Talk

Rooster A: "This egg is too small."
Rooster B: "And it's not round enough."
Rooster C: "The shell isn't red, either."
Mother Hen: "Let's see you guys try and lay one!"

## 论 蛋

公鸡甲:"这蛋太小了。"

公鸡乙:"也不够圆。"

公鸡丙:"蛋壳不红。"

母鸡:"你们下一个试试!"

## 94. Admiration

"What opinion do the people have of me?"
"They all admire you."
"They admire my position, my daring, or my eloquence?"
"None of the above. They admire your secretary."

### 羡 慕

"人们对我有什么议论吗?"

"他们都很羡慕你。"

"是羡慕我的职务、魄力还是口才?"

"不,他们羡慕你的秘书。"

## 95. Mistaken

Mother: "How much for a pound of this knitting wool?"
Daughter: "What are you blind? Can't you see for yourself?"
Mother: "What do you mean speaking to me like that?"
Daughter: "Oh, sorry. I thought I was still at work in the store."

## 错 了

母亲:"这毛线多少钱一斤呀?"

女儿:"你没长眼睛? 不会自己看!"

母亲:"你怎么这样说话呀?"

女儿:"哎呀,错了! 我还以为在商店里呢!"

## 96. Nightshift Steamed Bread

"How come the steamed bread is so black today."
"It was made by the nightshift."

### 夜班馒头

"今天的馒头怎么这么黑?"
"夜班做的。"

## 97. Taking Care of Big Things

"At home, I take care of big things, and my wife little things."
"What counts as a big thing."
"In the several decades I've been married, it hasn't occurred yet."

### 管 大 事

"在家里，我管大事，她管小事。"

"什么事算大事？"

"结婚几十年来还没有发生过呢！"

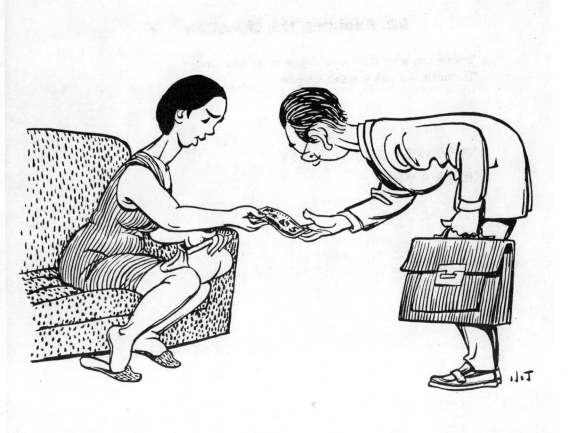

## 98. Avoiding the Question

"Excuse me, what does your boyfriend do for a living?"
"His uncle is a rich overseas Chinese."

## 答非所问

"请问你的男朋友是干什么工作的？"
"他舅舅是华侨。"

## 99. Promise of Love

Woman: "Will you still love me when I'm old?"
Man: "Will I *still* love you *when* you're old?"

### 爱 的 诺 言

女:"等将来我老了的时候,你还爱我吗?"
男:"还用等吗?!"

## 100. A Father's Occupation

On the first day of kindergarten, the teacher asked her students what their fathers do for a living. One student answered, "My father holds meetings. I always hear him tell my mother, 'Today I have a meeting, tomorrow I have a meeting, the day after tomorrow I also have a meeting....' "

## 爸爸的职业

幼儿园开学的那天,阿姨问起小朋友们家长的职业。

一个小朋友说:"我爸爸是'开会的'。我老听爸爸对妈妈说,今天开会,明天开会,后天还要开会……"

# List of Titles

1. Leave Together — 12
   一起走
2. Don't Always Arrive Late — 14
   别老迟到
3. Wedding Wear — 16
   婚 服
4. So Thin — 18
   瘦的原因
5. The Mirror in the Exhibition Parlour — 20
   展厅里的镜子
6. Pulse — 22
   脉 搏
7. The Wife's Not Home — 24
   妻子不在家
8. Imported Watch — 26
   进口时间
9. True Gentleman — 28
   "真君子"
10. Theatrical Performance — 30
    剧场效果
11. The Honorarium — 32
    稿 酬

12. World Record  34
    世界纪录

13. Vision  36
    视　力

14. Three Idiots  38
    三个笨蛋

15. I Laughed Last Year  40
    我去年笑过了

16. Not Completely Copied  42
    不是全抄

17. Boredom  44
    无　聊

18. Throw Out the Cat  46
    扔　猫

19. Teacher Is Not as Good as I Am  48
    老师不如我

20. Stamp a Seal  50
    盖　章

21. Alterations  52
    没关系

22. Observations  54
    考察的体会

23. Five-Step Snake  56
    五步蛇

24. Giving Fish  58
    送　鱼

| | |
|---|---|
| 25. Efficiency<br>效　率 | 60 |
| 26. After Losing the Cat<br>丢猫以后 | 62 |
| 27. Persistence<br>贵在坚持 | 64 |
| 28. New Law to Protect Forests<br>护林新法 | 66 |
| 29. Installing the Doorbell<br>装门铃 | 68 |
| 30. Steps to Reform<br>改革的措施 | 70 |
| 31. Dealing with Complaints<br>意见的处理 | 72 |
| 32. Solving the Problem of Meetings and Documents<br>解决"文山会海" | 74 |
| 33. Habits Become the Norm<br>习惯成自然 | 76 |
| 34. No Vacancies—Vacancies<br>无房——有房 | 78 |
| 35. The Friends of the Head of Department X<br>X长的朋友 | 80 |
| 36. Go to Work<br>上班去 | 82 |
| 37. Clap Your Hands<br>鼓　掌 | 84 |

| | |
|---|---|
| 38. Goods Coming at the Same Time<br>同时进的货 | 86 |
| 39. Conserve Electricity, Buy Glasses<br>省电买眼镜 | 88 |
| 40. Misunderstanding<br>误会 | 90 |
| 41. Choose Your Own Height<br>选择你的标准身高 | 92 |
| 42. The Worried Husband<br>粗心的丈夫 | 94 |
| 43. Family Law<br>"家法" | 96 |
| 44. Visit the Home<br>家访 | 98 |
| 45. Taking a Break<br>休息的时候 | 100 |
| 46. The Difference Between Inside and Out<br>内外有别 | 102 |
| 47. The Art of Hypnosis<br>催眠新术 | 104 |
| 48. Worried<br>担心 | 106 |
| 49. Scenes at the Hospital<br>某医院见闻 | 108 |
| 50. Think of a Way<br>想办法 | 110 |

51. Overlooked                                      112
    疏　忽

52. Misfortune                                      114
    不　幸

53. Thanks for the Advice                           116
    谢谢指教

54. Giving Out Bonus Money                          118
    发奖金

55. Photos                                          120
    照　像

56. Measuring Height                                122
    量身高

57. Ready-Made Pits to Plant Trees                  124
    现坑种树

58. Still Effective                                 126
    仍然有效

59. Looking for a Husband                           128
    找对象

60. Know Whom to Lie to                             130
    看对象撒谎

61. Stay Out of Other's Business                    132
    少管闲事

62. All Different Kinds                             134
    花样繁多

63. Not Always                                      136
    并非老是

64. Lingering Fear  138
　　心有余悸

65. Father and Son  140
　　父与子

66. No Future  142
　　没出息

67. After Marriage  144
　　婚　后

68. Facial Hair  146
　　嘴上毛

69. Washing Machine  148
　　洗衣机

70. Deciphering a Love Letter  150
　　"详"情书

71. Flies  152
　　苍　蝇

72. Doctor's Orders  154
　　医　嘱

73. "Yes" Man  156
　　唯唯诺诺的人

74. Looking Like a Scholar  158
　　显示学问

75. Whoever Returns Home First  160
　　谁先回到家

76. High and Low Voices  162
　　高低音

217

77. Heroes Meet                                    164
    英雄所见

78. Disappearance                                  166
    消　失

79. Mistaken                                       168
    弄错了

80. Way to Conserve Electricity                    170
    节电法

81. Applying for Welfare                           172
    申请生活补助

82. Wrong Place                                    174
    错　位

83. Division of Labour                             176
    分　工

84. Air of a Leader                                178
    领导的气派

85. Confused Father                                180
    胡涂爸爸

86. Unwilling to Be Heartbroken                    182
    不愿伤"心"

87. Exchange of Experiences                        184
    经验交流

88. The Old Man Gives Up His Seat                  186
    老大爷让座

89. Old Legend, New Interpretation                 188
    旧俗新解

| | |
|---|---|
| 90. Each Has His Own Gains<br>各有所获 | 190 |
| 91. In Writing<br>书　面 | 192 |
| 92. Incognito Inspection<br>"微服"私访 | 194 |
| 93. Egg Talk<br>论　蛋 | 196 |
| 94. Admiration<br>羡　慕 | 198 |
| 95. Mistaken<br>错　了 | 200 |
| 96. Nightshift Steamed Bread<br>夜班馒头 | 202 |
| 97. Taking Care of Big Things<br>管大事 | 204 |
| 98. Avoiding the Question<br>答非所问 | 206 |
| 99. Promise of Love<br>爱的诺言 | 208 |
| 100. A Father's Occupation<br>爸爸的职业 | 210 |

图书在版编目(CIP)数据

今趣集/丁聪编绘

－北京：新世界出版社，1993(2000.2 重印)

ISBN 7－80005－112－9

Ⅰ．今… Ⅱ．丁… Ⅲ．漫画-作品集-中国-现代 Ⅳ．J228.2

中英对照

# 今 趣 集

丁 聪 编绘

\*

新世界出版社出版
（北京百万庄路24号）
新华书店北京发行所发行
北京新华印刷厂印刷
850×1168(毫米) 1/24 开本
1993年第一版 2000年第四次印刷
ISBN 7-80005-112-9/J·048
定价：24.00元